SOLVE IT WITH SCIENCE

FRAUDS AND COUNTERFEITS

PAUL MASON

A⁺

Smart Apple Media

This book has been published in cooperation with Arcturus Publishing Limited.

The right of Paul Mason to be identified as the author of this work has been asserted by him in accordance with the Copyright, Designs and Patents Act 1988.

Series concept: Alex Woolf
Editor and picture researcher: Alex Woolf
Designer: Tall Tree

Copyright © 2009 Arcturus Publishing Limited

Published in the United States by Smart Apple Media
P.O. Box 3263, Mankato, Minnesota 56002

Printed in China

Library of Congress Cataloging-in-Publication Data

Mason, Paul.
    Frauds and counterfeits / Paul Mason.
       p. cm. – (Solve it with science)
    Includes bibliographical references and index.
    ISBN 978-1-59920-329-4 (hardcover)
    1. Fraud–Juvenile literature. 2. Counterfeits and counterfeiting–Juvenile literature. I. Title.
    HV6691.M287 2010
    363.25'963–dc22
                                                2009001483

9 8 7 6 5 4 3 2 1

Picture credits:
Corbis: 4 (Michael Kooren/Reuters), 8 (Bettmann), 9 (Hugo Philpott/epa), 10 (Bettmann), 11 (Bettmann), 38 (Peter Burian).
Getty: 14 (Maurice Ambler/Stringer), 20 (Hulton Archive/Stringer), 25 (George Rodger/Time & Life Pictures), 40 (Ben Martin/Time Life Pictures), 42 *top* (Indranil Mukherjee/AFP).
PA Photos: 28 (Thomas Grimm/AP), 30 (Kurt Strumpf/AP), 32 (Daniel Luna/AP), 35 (David McHugh/PA Archive), 36 (David McHugh/PA Archive).
Rex Features: cover right and 24 (Roger-Viollet), 34.
Ridges and Furrows: 37 *fingerprints*
Science Photo Library: 6 (Sheila Terry), 7 (Volker Steger), 12 (John Reader), 13, 17, 22 (Ria Novosti), 23 (Pasieka), 26 (Volker Steger), 27 (Volker Steger), 31 (Andrew Lambert Photography), 33 (David Parker), 41 (Andrew Syred), 43 (Hank Morgan).
Shutterstock: cover *pen and ink* (Lorenzo Mondo), cover *text on parchment* (Kenneth V Pilon), 5 (Lorelyn Medina), 21 (yellowj), 29 (Marek Slusarczyk), 39 (Maksim Shmeljov).
TopFoto: 16 (Fortean), 18 (Fortean), 19 (Fortean).

Every attempt has been made to clear copyright. Should there be any inadvertent omission, please apply to the publisher for rectification.

All words in **bold** may be found in the glossary on pages 46–47.

CONTENTS

INTRODUCTION

In 2006, a painting by Jackson Pollock was bought at auction for $140 million. The sale made it the most expensive painting ever sold. With works of art going for prices like that, it's not surprising that dishonest people have sometimes been tempted to copy paintings and other valuable items, and then sell them.

Geert Jan Jansen, a master art forger, stands in front of some of his works. According to experts, his copies of great works are barely distinguishable from the originals.

COUNTERFEITING

Counterfeiters are people who make a convincing copy or version of something, then pretend it's the original item. In the 19th century, **counterfeit** money was a large problem. The problem still exists today, but requires advanced technology as there are many special features on bills. People have also counterfeited paintings, photographs, and official documents.

FRAUD—TURNING COUNTERFEITS INTO MONEY

Fraud means tricking people in order to make money or for some other benefit. An example of fraud would be persuading someone to buy a counterfeit painting that the customer believes is real. When criminals sell counterfeit paintings—or documents, papers, or even stories —they are committing fraud.

FORENSIC INVESTIGATIONS

Counterfeiters go to great lengths to make their fakes convincing. One painter spent years trying to find a way to make his paintings look hundreds of years old. A forger of old documents mixed his own inks, using only ingredients that were available in the 1800s. Often the only way these counterfeits can be discovered is through a forensic investigation. A forensic investigation uses science to prove that the item is a fake and to figure out who produced it.

WANT TO BE A FORENSIC INVESTIGATOR?

Forensic investigators are trained scientists. Most have a college degree in biology or chemistry. A few people start out as forensic assistants and then do extra part-time education while working. Trainee investigators learn through on-the-job training. They work on real cases and are also taught in classrooms by experienced investigators. After about 18 months' training, they become qualified forensic investigators.

Special safety features in money make it difficult to counterfeit.

REPEATING RESULTS

One of the basic techniques of a forensic investigation is repeating results. For example, if ink mixed in the forensic lab is exactly the same as ink used in a counterfeit document, the investigators can be sure that the two inks were mixed in the same way. If they find the same ink-mixing chemicals in the basement of one of the suspects, they know who to arrest!

Under normal light (top) this check looks fine. But ultraviolet light (below) reveals that someone has added a zero to make it 60 instead of six.

PHYSICAL EVIDENCE

In some crimes, physical evidence helps investigators. The best-known example is when a criminal leaves fingerprints behind at the crime scene. This allows investigators to prove that the criminal was there. There are other kinds of physical evidence. For example:

- Hair, skin, or other tiny traces of a criminal's body might be left at the scene. The **DNA** these contain is like a fingerprint, which can be used to identify the criminal.
- A person might claim to be the long-lost son of a rich man. Comparing the DNA of the two will prove whether the claim is true or not.

CHEMICAL TESTING

Forensic investigators often use chemical tests in their work. For example, they might use chemical tests to see how old a piece of paper is. If a document is claimed to date from 1812, yet after tests it turns out to be just 30 years old, investigators can be sure it's counterfeit.

OTHER TECHNIQUES

Forensic investigators have plenty more tricks up their sleeves! They also have methods of testing whether or not handwriting, photos, and voices are genuine. They can use geology (the study of rocks and soils) to test the authenticity of **fossils** and X-rays to peer beneath the surface of paintings. The development of computers since the 1970s has greatly sped up the work of forensic investigators.

A forensic investigator uses a microscope to examine a forged painting.

TYPES OF FORENSIC SCIENCE

Many forensic scientists specialize in a particular kind of investigation. These include:

- **Crime scene investigation**
- **Document examination**
- **Fire investigation**
- **Firearms examination**
- **Forensic imaging**
- **Computer investigation**

THE SHAKESPEARE FORGERIES

Nearly everyone has heard of the playwright William Shakespeare. But what we know for certain about his life can be written on the back of an envelope. Examples of Shakespeare's actual handwriting survive on only a few scraps of paper. This makes any documents written by Shakespeare extremely valuable.

William Henry Ireland, the famous forger of Shakespearean documents and manuscripts

NEW SHAKESPEARE DOCUMENTS

Imagine the excitement in 1794 when William Henry Ireland told his father that he had found an example of Shakespeare's signature. William Henry's father was thrilled—he was a collector of Shakespearean documents. The only trouble was, William Henry had forged the signature! He didn't stop there—he went on to "discover" letters, copies of plays and then, in 1795, a whole new play. Soon, the Ireland family was making a lot of money from the forged documents.

The new play was quickly **denounced** as a forgery. Leading Shakespeare scholars lined up to say it could not be genuine. A theater planned to perform it on April Fools' Day.

EXPOSING THE FORGERIES

One of those who claimed that the documents were fake was a lawyer named Edmond Malone. He used several forensic techniques to expose the forgeries:

- Orthography—the style of handwriting used in the documents, which had been different in Shakespeare's day.
- Handwriting analysis—see page 29.
- Phraseology—the forged papers used different phrases and expressions from those used by Shakespeare.

In 1796, William Henry admitted that the documents had all been forged. He had forged every single document himself. Remarkably, he had been just 21 at the time.

The First Folio, printed in 1623, is the earliest known version of Shakespeare's works. Ireland claimed to have found original manuscripts written by Shakespeare himself.

WATERMARKS

Malone's evidence included the watermarks on the papers. Although the plays were written on paper from the correct time period, each sheet had a different watermark. Malone argued that if they had all been taken from a stack of writers' paper, the sheets would all have had the same watermark. Instead of this, they must have been used from the endpapers of lots of different books.

THE CARDIFF GIANT

During the 1870s, tens of thousands of people paid money to see what were apparently the remains of a 10 foot (3 m) giant man. But did giants ever really walk the Earth—or was the Cardiff Giant a fake and a fraud?

WHAT WAS THE GIANT?

The Cardiff Giant was a fairground attraction in the United States during the 1870s and later. The giant was said to be the **petrified** remains of a man. It had been discovered buried near the town of Cardiff, New York.

The Cardiff Giant was discovered in 1869 by workers digging a well.

MAKING MONEY FROM THE GIANT

Visitors paid to see the giant because it appeared to offer proof of a passage in the Bible. The passage suggested that giants had once walked the Earth. The giant was such a popular attraction that the famous showman P.T. Barnum tried to buy it. When the owners refused, Barnum made a **replica** and showed that instead!

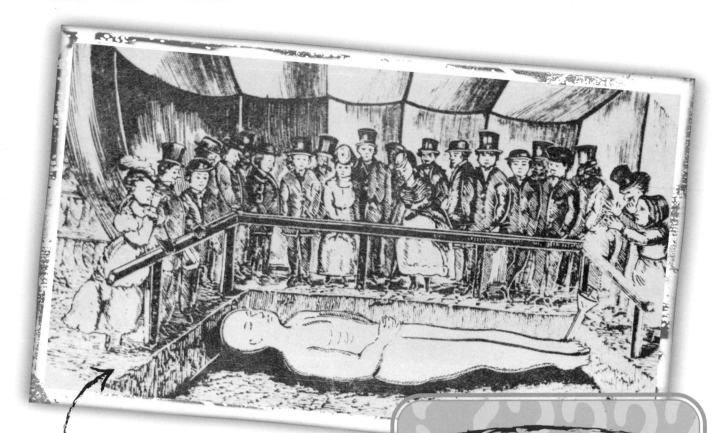

Even after the giant had been unmasked as a fake, people still kept paying to see it! They called it "Old Hoaxey."

WAS THE GIANT REAL?

If giants did once walk the Earth, the Cardiff Giant wasn't proof of it! Investigators found that the giant had been carved from a block of limestone, then stained with acids and **colorants** to make it seem old. The "skin" had then been beaten with knitting needles to make dents that looked like the pores in a person's skin!

PROVING THE GIANT A FAKE

A paleontologist from Yale University named Othniel C. Marsh examined the Cardiff Giant. Marsh pointed out that chisel marks were visible on the stone. This showed that the giant wasn't even a very old statue. If the giant had been buried for a long time, these marks would have worn away. Marsh proved that the giant was actually a modern fake, which had been buried only recently.

THE MISSING LINK?

For many years scientists, have thought that humans and apes share a common **ancestor**. If this theory was correct, an ape-man or man-ape must once have existed. But evidence of such a creature had never been found. Then, in 1912, the world was rocked by the apparent discovery of the "missing link" between apes and men.

A reconstruction of the Piltdown Man skull. The skull was given a scientific name, Eoanthropus dawsoni, and entered the science textbooks.

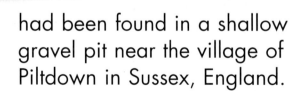

HEADLINES AROUND THE WORLD

"The earliest man?" asked the headline in one newspaper. There was a similarly excited response all around the world. But what had been discovered? It was **fossilized** skull fragments, a jawbone and other remains, including teeth. They seemed to be from a creature that was part human, part ape. The remains had been found in a shallow gravel pit near the village of Piltdown in Sussex, England.

PILTDOWN MAN

The discoveries quickly became known as Piltdown Man. The skull and teeth looked similar to those of a human, but the jawbone was clearly ape-like. They seemed to belong to an early human ancestor from 500,000 years ago.

DOUBTS EMERGE

It wasn't long before a few experts began to question whether Piltdown Man was genuine. **Geologists** pointed out that the flint rocks where the remains had been discovered were nothing like 500,000 years old. One wrote: "the bones . . . might even represent a deliberate hoax . . . 'planted' in the gravel bed to fool the scientists."

Charles Dawson (left), who first discovered the Piltdown site, with Arthur Smith Woodward of the British Museum. They are at the gravel pit where Piltdown Man was first unearthed.

GEOLOGY AND THE AGE OF ROCKS

Rocks are formed by natural forces that crush them together and make them hard. The crushing happens in a variety of ways and over varying periods of time, which gives different rocks their characteristics. Geologists (people who study rocks) are able to tell from these characteristics how old a rock is likely to be. Any fossil found within that rock must be the same age—unless it has been deliberately placed there to fool people.

A paleontologist demonstrates that the Piltdown skull is made up of the remains of a man and an orangutan.

JAWBONE CONCERNS

Other concerns existed about Piltdown Man's authenticity. The section of the jaw that normally connects with the skull was missing. Without it, it was impossible to be sure that the skull and jawbone came from the same creature.

THE FRAUD IS UNCOVERED

During the 1950s, those who had doubted whether Piltdown Man was genuine were proved correct. Several pieces of evidence emerged that showed that the bones were a fraud:

- When examined under a microscope, it was clear that the teeth had been ground down to change their shape.
- Chemical tests showed that, far from being 500,000 years old, the jawbone and teeth were modern. The jawbone came from an orangutan!
- More tests showed that the bones had been made to look old using a combination of acid and iron. This was convincing because bones that have been buried absorb iron from the soil.

By 1954, there was no doubt that Piltdown Man was a fraud. One newspaper called it "The biggest scientific hoax of the century."

WHODUNNIT?

One mystery remained: who had faked the Piltdown remains? Various culprits have been suggested, including the detective-story writer Arthur Conan Doyle, who lived nearby. No one will ever know for sure, but it seems most likely to have been the "discoverer" of the remains, Charles Dawson. In 2003, a book suggested that at least 33 of Dawson's other archaeological discoveries had been faked. It is unlikely that his Piltdown discoveries were the work of *another* hoaxer.

REPRODUCING RESULTS

Sometimes forensic investigators test a theory about how a fake was produced by producing a copy of the fake themselves. This is what happened with Piltdown Man: Professor J.S. Weiner used a chimpanzee tooth, filed it down into a more human shape, then stained it to make it look old. The result looked just like the Piltdown teeth—which suggested they too had been faked.

15

THE COTTINGLEY FAIRIES

It would be hard to convince people today that you had seen fairies at the bottom of your garden. But in 1919, people were more willing to believe such a story—especially when it was supported by photographic evidence.

THE FAIRIES APPEAR

This story begins in summer 1917. Two girls in a garden in Cottingley, Yorkshire, United Kingdom, took a photograph that seemed to prove the existence of fairies. The photo showed the younger girl, ten-year-old Frances Griffiths, facing a group of tiny, flying fairies. Within a short time, Frances and her cousin, Elsie Wright, had taken another photo showing fairies.

Frances Griffiths with the fairies, taken by Elsie Wright in July 1917.

WERE THE PHOTOS REAL?

At first the girls' family thought the photos were interesting enough to be passed around among friends, but no more. Then, in 1919, the photos caught the public's attention, including that of Arthur Conan Doyle, famous creator of the fictional detective Sherlock Holmes.

An expert examined the photos to see if they had been faked. He reported: "These two negatives are entirely genuine, unfaked photos . . . In my opinion they are both straight, untouched pictures."

A second examination of the photos, by experts from the Kodak company, also suggested that they had not been tampered with. However, the Kodak report added that, "as fairies couldn't be true, the photographs must have been faked somehow."

A fake photograph of Arthur Conan Doyle with ghostly figures above his head. This fake is badly done, yet it managed to fool Conan Doyle himself.

PHOTO ANALYSIS

Experts analyze photos looking for evidence they have been faked. Among the things they look for are:

- **Objects with a hard edge instead of a slightly blurry one — this suggests that the objects have been cut out of another image and added later.**

- **Parts of the photo where the light falls in a different direction from the rest, for example a face with a shadow on the left, when all the other shadows are on the right.**

INVESTIGATING THE PHOTOS

If the photos hadn't been tampered with, how had the fairies ended up in them? Over the next 60 years, a long list of experts tried to unravel the mystery of the photos. Many of them agreed with Arthur Wright, Elsie's father, that the photos were probably fakes. But like Arthur, who had searched for evidence that the photos were not real, no one was able to prove it. The most Elsie would admit was that the photos were "figments of our imaginations."

SOLVING THE RIDDLE

By 1976 a TV reporter thought he had found the answer to how the fraud had been pulled off: the fairies *were* in the photo, but they *weren't* fairies. He managed to produce very similar results using paper cut-outs of fairies, held upright by wire.

Elsie Wright and a fairy, photographed by Frances Griffiths. One expert pointed out that the fairies had very fashionable Parisian haircuts, which seemed unlikely for Yorkshire fairies.

ELSIE CONFESSES

Despite the TV reporter's efforts, plenty of people refused to accept that the fairies weren't real. The story ran and ran until, in 1983, the truth finally emerged. Elsie Wright admitted that the "fairies" were actually cut-out paper figures, secured to the ground using hatpins.

In a twist to the story, Elsie maintained that although the photos were faked, she and her cousin really had seen fairies at the bottom of the garden.

TRIAL AND ERROR

The riddle of the Cottingley fairies was finally solved using trial and error. The investigator tried various techniques until he found one that produced the same results as had been achieved in the original photos. Forensic investigators often use this technique. For example:

• They fire bullets from a gun to see if they match bullets taken from a crime scene.

• They use a particular kind of knife to make a cut, to see if it was the kind used in a crime.

Elsie Wright, pictured in 1983 with a paper cut-out fairy, shows how she and Frances Griffiths faked their photographs 70 years before.

ANASTASIA—THE LAST RUSSIAN ROYAL?

The story of Anastasia is a murder mystery with a difference. Was the Russian princess murdered in 1917 —or did she somehow survive the massacre of her family and end up living in the United States?

Anna Anderson, pictured in 1926. Could she have been Princess Anastasia?

MURDER OF THE ROYAL FAMILY

Anastasia's father was Tsar Nicholas II, ruler of Russia. In 1917, he was overthrown in a **communist** revolution. The communists imprisoned Nicholas and his family, including Anastasia. Then it seemed that anti-communist forces might rescue them. To prevent this, the family's guards herded them together and shot them. Their bodies were buried in an unmarked grave.

AFTER THE REVOLUTION

Many Russian **aristocrats** fled to Europe and the United States after the revolution. Some claimed to be surviving members of the royal family. Most were quickly exposed as frauds who hoped to claim the family fortune from its Swiss bank accounts. But one woman who claimed to be Anastasia even managed to convince people who had known Anastasia before the revolution. The woman's name was Anna Anderson.

COMPARING PHOTOGRAPHS

Not everyone was convinced that Anna was Anastasia. In 1927, Professor Mark Bischoff of the Institute of Police Science in Lausanne, Switzerland, decided to carry out some tests to see if he could prove her identity. He compared photos of Anna with those of Anastasia. Bischoff focused on the right ear of both women, since no two people's ears are exactly the same. He noticed some differences between the two.

Everyone's ears are unique, making them a potentially useful means of identification.

EAR IDENTIFICATION

Like fingerprints, everyone's ears are different. The first person to suggest this was French criminologist Alphonse Bertillon in 1883. In 1906, Czech doctor R. Imhofer wrote a piece on identifying people by their ears. Later in 1964, an American named Alfred Iannarelli published a book on ear identification. Iannarelli proposed a system of classifying ears according to certain characteristics. Ear identification can be useful for individuals who cannot be fingerprinted due to diseases of the skin, in cases of mass casualties, or to distinguish the difference between multiples, such as twins.

DISCOVERY OF THE BODIES

Despite Bischoff's work, many people continued to believe Anna was Anastasia. Then in 1979, geologist Alexander Avdonin discovered the grave of the Russian royal family. Avdonin kept his discovery quiet, but by the 1990s word of the grave became public. In 1991, a team of experts **exhumed**, or dug up the bodies, and confirmed that they belonged to the royal family. But one mystery remained: none of the bones in the grave belonged to Anastasia or her brother Alexei. It seemed for a while that Anna Anderson might really be Anastasia.

A forensic scientist examines the skeletons of the Russian royal family after they were exhumed in 1991.

THE DNA TRAIL

Anna Anderson had died in 1984, but a **tissue sample** containing her **DNA** had been kept. Scientists compared Anna's DNA with DNA taken from Prince Philip, husband of Queen Elizabeth II of England. Prince Philip's grandmother had been Anastasia's aunt. If Anna had been Anastasia, DNA tests would show that she and Prince Philip were related. Anna's DNA was also compared to samples taken from the family's grave in Russia. Both tests came back with the same result: Anna Anderson was not a member of the Russian royal family, so she could not have been Anastasia.

WHO WAS ANNA ANDERSON?

Later DNA tests showed that Anna was actually from a family called Schanzkowski. She came from a part of Poland called Pomerania, and not from Russia at all.

A DNA molecule. DNA is made up of two long strands twisted into a spiral shape called a double helix. DNA contains sections, called genes. These carry the information that determines all the characteristics of an individual.

DNA TESTING

DNA is a chemical molecule inside every cell in our bodies. DNA is shaped a bit like a twisted rope ladder. The ladder is made up of six different types of matter. The exact order in which these six things join together is what gives us our unique characteristics. The order is different in every human being, except identical twins. By examining DNA, scientists can tell one person from another. They can look at two separate samples and say whether they come from the same person—or even whether they came from people of the same family.

THE MAN WHO CONNED THE NAZIS

A high-ranking **Nazi** called Hermann Göring was famous for his love of valuable art. Göring was one of the most powerful men in Europe during **World War II**. He could easily demand someone's imprisonment or even execution. Even so, one Dutch forger dared to fool Göring into buying one of his fake paintings.

THE FAKE VERMEER

The painting Göring bought was supposedly by a famous Dutch artist called Jan Vermeer. Today, Vermeer's paintings are sold for

Han van Meegeren was one of the greatest art forgers of the 20th century.

tens of millions of dollars. Even in the 1930s and 1940s, they were very valuable. Göring actually "bought" the Vermeer by swapping it for 200 other Dutch paintings. He had **looted** these from the museums and art galleries of Europe. He had no idea that he had been conned. Göring's new painting was a valueless fake.

TRACING THE SELLER

During World War II, the Nazis controlled most of Europe by force, including Holland. When the war ended, many people wanted to punish those who had worked with the Nazis. Among those the Dutch wanted to punish was whoever had sold a valuable Vermeer to Göring. The sale was traced to a man called Han van Meegeren. Van Meegeren was arrested and put in jail.

THE FRAUD IS UNCOVERED

Van Meegeren would have faced the death sentence if found guilty of **collaboration**. He was forced to admit that the painting had not been a Vermeer at all. In fact, Van Meegeren himself had painted it—along with quite a few other "Vermeers."

FAKING OLD PAINTINGS

Faking a painting to look as if it had been made in the 1600s, when Vermeer was alive, is not easy. How did Van Meegeren do it?

- He invented a way of imitating the cracked surface of old paintings by baking the paintings in an oven. No one knows how many prototypes went up in smoke before he achieved the desired result!

- He mixed his paints from raw ingredients, just as Vermeer had.

Han van Meegeren works on a new "Vermeer": Young Christ Teaching in the Temple.

A forensic investigator uses a needle to remove a tiny paint sample from a painting. A chemical analysis of the sample will determine whether the painting is a forgery.

INVESTIGATING THE PAINTINGS

Was Van Meegeren telling the truth, or was he just trying to escape punishment for working with the Nazis? A special commission was appointed to investigate. Van Meegeren helped the commission, revealing many of the secrets of his forger's art.

After nine months' work, the commission gave its report: the paintings were fakes, and had probably been painted by Van Meegeren. Among the evidence:

- Chemical analysis of paints revealed that they contained tiny amounts of modern chemicals that had not even been invented when Vermeer was painting.

- X-rays revealed that under Van Meegeren's paintings there were traces of earlier paintings on the **canvases**. Van Meegeren had scraped these off in order to be able to paint on canvases from the 1600s.

THE TRIAL OF VAN MEEGEREN

Once the commission reported that the paintings were fakes, the charges against Van Meegeren were changed. He was accused of forgery instead of collaboration. By now Van Meegeren had become a hero to many Dutch people. They loved the fact that he had conned the Nazis. Van

Meegeren himself pointed out that his actions had pried 200 valuable Dutch paintings from Göring's clutches. He pleaded guilty and was given a light sentence. But Van Meegeren died of a heart attack before setting foot in jail.

This is an X-ray of a painting by the artist Titian (1514–1576). The X-ray reveals how the artist developed the painting, for example changing the position of the woman's head. It proves that the painting is genuine.

X-RAY ANALYSIS

X-ray analysis can be used to discover if there is anything underneath the surface layer of a painting. X-rays are able to pass through solid matter in a way that light cannot. The rays are affected by the thickness of the matter they are passing through. Because of this, thicker areas show up lighter on the X-ray image. By comparing X-ray images of Van Meegeren's paintings with the visible outer layers, experts were able to see traces of older paintings underneath.

27

THE HITLER DIARIES

Adolf Hitler was the infamous leader of **Nazi** Germany, blamed by many for causing the terrible death and destruction of **World War II**. He is recognized as one of the most influential men of the 20th century. It is therefore hard to exaggerate the shock and excitement caused by the announcement, in 1983, of the discovery of Hitler's diaries.

Gerd Heidemann holds up one of the diaries at a press conference in 1983.

DISCOVERY OF THE DIARIES

A German magazine, *Stern*, made the announcement. A wealthy collector of Nazi souvenirs named Dr. Fischer had offered the diaries to a journalist, Gerd Heidemann. Heidemann then offered them to *Stern*. Fischer claimed the diaries had been smuggled out of Berlin, Germany, at the end of the war. The plane carrying them had crashed near a village in East Germany. Fischer's brother, an East German general, had rescued the documents and kept them safe for years until the time was right to sell them.

THE BIG QUESTION

The big question *Stern* asked was, "Are these really Hitler's diaries?" If they were, the documents would be of enormous historical and commercial value. *Stern* brought in two handwriting experts to say whether the diaries were truly the work of Hitler. The experts compared pages from the diaries with other notes that Hitler had written. The experts agreed: the diaries were genuine. *Stern* immediately set about selling the story to other magazines and newspapers around the world.

Your handwriting, like your fingerprints, is unique to you.

HANDWRITING ANALYSIS

Everybody writes slightly differently. This means experts can compare two pieces of handwriting and say whether or not they have been written by the same person. Among the aspects the experts compare are:

- **The various parts of each letter. For example, does every "y" have a big loop underneath it? At what angle is the loop drawn?**

- **How the letters are formed overall. For example, is the letter "a" the same shape in both examples? Is the letter "t" always crossed in the same way?**

- **How the words are joined together. For example, are "t" and "h" always joined up?**

MR. NICE GUY?

The diaries seemed to show that Hitler was less unpleasant than people thought. For example, they suggested he had known little of *Kristallnacht*—a night in 1938 when his supporters smashed up and burned Jewish homes and businesses. Also, some events described in the diaries differed from other accepted historical accounts. Many people began to think that the diaries could not be genuine, whatever the handwriting experts said.

Hans Booms of the West German Federal Archives announces that the Hitler diaries are forgeries.

A BITTER ARGUMENT

A bitter argument soon developed between people who thought the diaries were Hitler's and those who said they could not be. To try to settle the matter, the German government ordered further tests. On May 6, 1983, the results were announced at a dramatic press conference: the diaries were a fake, the work of a forger.

CHEMICAL TESTING

Forensic scientists carried out a chemical analysis of the paper, glue, inks, and bindings. They found out what chemicals had been used to make each of these things. They quickly realized that some of the chemicals used in the paper, ink, and glue had only become available after the end of World War II. This proved that the paper on which the diaries were written had been made after Hitler was already dead. The diaries could not be genuine.

The forger turned out to be Dr. Fischer. "Fischer" was, in fact, Konrad Kujau, a petty criminal and fraud, who had written the diaries himself.

RED FACES ALL AROUND

The diaries's supporters were greatly embarrassed by the results. How had they been fooled? Mainly it was because they *wanted* to believe the diaries were genuine:

- Some Hitler supporters liked the less unpleasant version of him that the diaries "revealed."

- Some honest historians were so excited by the discovery that they made terrible mistakes.

- The magazine and newspaper editors who bought the story knew it could make them a lot of money.

Ink can be analyzed using paper chromatography. This process separates the ink into its constituent chemicals.

31

ARGENTINA'S STOLEN CHILDREN

Between 1976 and 1983, Argentina was ruled by a powerful military organization called the junta. The junta tried to crush anyone who opposed its ideas, using torture and death against its opponents. The junta even stole its opponents' children and secretly sent them to live with its supporters. That way, the children stood a better chance of growing up to be junta supporters, too.

THE SEARCH FOR MISSING CHILDREN AND PARENTS

For many years the full story of Argentina's stolen children was not known. But when the junta lost control of Argentina, the truth began to emerge. People were now free to search for their missing children, and children were able to look for their parents. Some 400 children had been stolen by the government. Since 1983, 77 have been reunited with their families.

The mothers of some of the stolen children hold a demonstration in Buenos Aires, the Argentinian capital, in 2003.

FIDELA MOREL
Y
ALBERTO HORACIO
GARCIA

SECUESTRADOS
EL 29 JULIO DE 1976

DNA IN FAMILIES

DNA is the genetic code for how we are put together. It determines our hair, eye, and skin color, our height, and all our other physical characteristics. It is like a fingerprint hidden in every cell in our bodies. The DNA of members of the same family is similar, which is why family members often look alike. It is even more similar if they are closely related. For example, the DNA of brothers and sisters is more similar than the DNA of cousins.

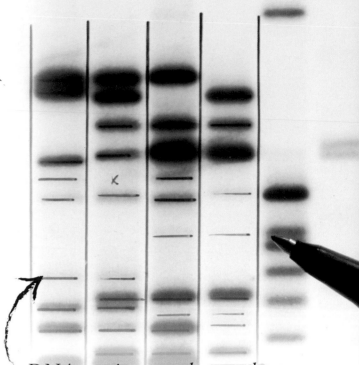

DNA testing can be used to prove family relationships. Each of these columns is the DNA "fingerprint" of a family member. As can be seen, the children (C) have some bands in common with their parents (M and F).

MARIA EUGENIA SAMPALLO

Maria Eugenia Sampallo's grandmother and brother had been looking for her since she and her parents had disappeared in 1977. Maria had always doubted that the couple who had brought her up were her real

parents. In 2000 she took part in a DNA test that aimed to reunite stolen children with their families. The test showed that Maria's "parents" were not actually related to her. The tests also enabled Maria to rediscover her grandmother and brother. Unfortunately, Maria's parents, who had been arrested in 1977, were never seen again.

THE CASE OF THE KILLER CONMAN

In 1990, a Canadian businessman named Albert Walker fled Canada to evade capture by the police. Walker was a conman, someone who tricked other people out of their money. The police wanted to arrest him for fraud. He fled and took his 15-year-old daughter with him. It was the beginning of a story of stolen identity that would end in tragedy six years later.

A NEW IDENTITY

Walker went to the UK, where he and his daughter lived under false names. But Walker needed a proper new identity. He obtained it from a man he befriended named Ronald Platt. Platt and his girlfriend wanted to move to Canada, so Walker bought them a one-way ticket as a present. Platt and his girlfriend set off for a new life in Canada. But before they left, Walker stole Platt's birth certificate and driver's license. This allowed Walker to live as Platt.

Canadian businessman and con artist Albert Walker

MYSTERY BODY

Six years later, fishermen off the coast of Devon, UK, found the body of a man caught up in their nets. At first the authorities had no idea who he was. The only clue was the expensive watch found on the body's wrist. When the police contacted the watchmaker, they discovered that the watch belonged to a man named Ronald Platt.

TRACKING DOWN RECORDS

Forensic investigations require a lot of patience. Investigators follow every lead, ruling out possibilities one by one. For example, they might collect hundreds of different fibers from a crime scene, but only one will have come from the coat of the criminal. Unless every fiber is recorded, the important one might not be noticed. It was this painstaking approach, tracking down every detail, which helped identify Ronald Platt from the watch he was wearing.

Superintendant Phil Sincock of the Devon and Cornwall Police holds the Rolex watch found on the body of Ronald Platt.

Albert Walker murdered Ronald Platt on his yacht, Lady Jane, *shown here under police guard during Walker's trial.*

PLATT'S RETURN

Ronald Platt had gone to live in Canada—so what was his body doing in the sea off the coast of England? In fact, Platt had run out of money and had gotten tired of his life in Canada. After three years he returned home. Walker, who had been using Platt's identity, knew that there wasn't room in the UK for two Ronald Platts. He decided to get the real

Ronald Platt out of the way once and for all. Walker invited Platt on a sailing trip, then killed him. Walker tipped the body over the side of the boat and sailed off. Little did he know that the police would soon be hot on his trail.

PROVING WALKER GUILTY

Among Platt's belongings, the police discovered Walker's cell phone number. Then they found that Walker had a yacht **moored** in Devon—near where Platt's body was found. They quickly discovered two crucial clues:

- The yacht was equipped with a **GPS** navigation system. The police looked into the system's memory. They found that on the day Platt died, the yacht had been very close to where his body was later found.

- A plastic bag on the yacht had Platt's fingerprints on it. This showed that he had probably been on the boat.

Faced with this evidence, Walker's daughter Sheena **testified** against her father. She claimed that she had only gone along with him because he had **hypnotized** her.

In June 1998, a **jury** took less than two hours to find Albert Walker guilty of murder. He was sentenced to life imprisonment.

FINGERPRINT IDENTIFICATION

Fingerprint identification is one of the main ways for forensic investigators to prove that someone was at the scene of a crime. Fingerprints have three key shapes:

- **Loops**
- **Whorls**
- **Arches**

The way these shapes develop is slightly different in every human being, meaning that none of us has the same fingerprints.

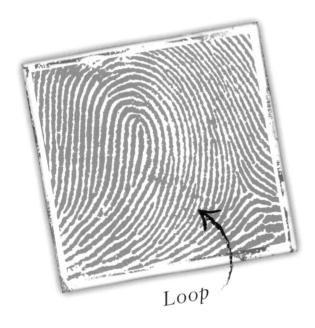

Loop

Whorl

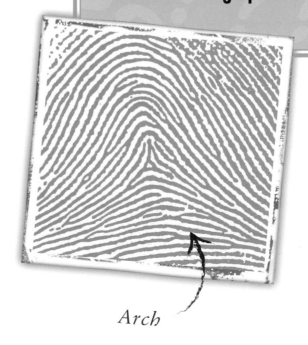

Arch

THE HOFMANN FORGERIES

This is a story of talking salamanders, angels, car bombs, and one of the world's greatest forgers. It is the story of how a set of forgeries was sold not to one person or even a few specialty collectors, but to a whole religion.

THE MORMON CHURCH DECEIVED

The Church of Jesus Christ of Latter-Day Saints (often called the Mormon Church) was founded in 1830. Documents from the Church's early days are highly valued by its leaders. During the 1980s, the Church bought many old documents from a man named Mark Hofmann. They included:

- Papers linked to the Book of Mormon, one of the religion's central texts;

- Papers that suggested the wrong person had led the religion after its founder was murdered;

- An old letter claiming that the religion's founder practiced magic and had once met a talking **salamander** that then turned into an angel.

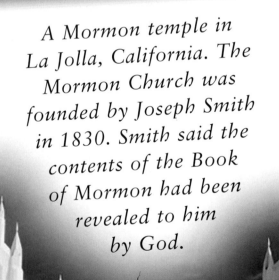

A Mormon temple in La Jolla, California. The Mormon Church was founded by Joseph Smith in 1830. Smith said the contents of the Book of Mormon had been revealed to him by God.

Forensic investigators look at the physical parts of an old document—its paper and ink—as well as the language and handwriting, in order to check whether it is genuine.

This last document, the "salamander letter," made people suspect that Hofmann's papers were forgeries. Hofmann denied that this was the case—but events would soon take a dramatic turn.

THE SALT LAKE CITY BOMBINGS

In October 1985, document collector Steve Christensen was killed by a bomb in Salt Lake City, Utah, home of the Mormon Church. Another bomb killed Kathy Sheets, wife of Christensen's former employer. The next day a third bomb went off in Hofmann's car, badly injuring him. When police went to Hofmann's house, they found evidence that he was a master forger and a not-so-successful bomb-maker.

PROVING OLD DOCUMENTS

Several forensic tests convinced the Mormon Church that the documents they bought from Hofmann were originals, not fakes:

- The paper on which the documents were written or printed was the right age.

- The language and spelling were consistent with the period when the Church was founded.

- The handwriting matched known examples of handwriting by the people who were said to have written the documents.

HOW WAS THE MORMON CHURCH FOOLED?

The Mormon Church was fooled because Hofmann was such a skillful, careful forger. He always used old paper. He often used the blank **endpapers** of old books or added his forgeries to genuine documents. Hofmann also learned to make inks that could not be distinguished from those of the time. Finally, he was highly skilled at imitating other people's handwriting.

THE BOMB ATTACKS

Steve Christensen had helped organize a loan for Hofmann, who was severely in debt. In return, Hofmann promised to offer Christensen rare documents written by one of the early **apostles** of the Mormon Church. Hofmann did not have the documents and had no time to forge them. As pressure from Christensen started to build, Hofmann decided to murder him.

Master forger Mark Hofmann displays a first edition of the Book of Mormon.

Hofmann is in prison, serving a life sentence for murder. His forgeries, though, are still out there causing problems for collectors of rare documents. The trouble is, the forgeries are so good that only very detailed forensic tests can expose them. These tests would destroy parts of the document. Very few collectors are willing to submit their expensive documents to such tests.

INK AND PAPER TESTS

Mark Hofmann's forgeries were so good that special forensic tests had to be invented to uncover them. Investigators already knew that the paper and ink used in making the documents came from the right time. So the forensic investigators looked instead at the absorption of the ink by the paper. Ink is absorbed into paper over time, and both the ink and the paper change as a result. The investigators developed a new test to figure out how long the ink had been on the paper. By this means, they were able to prove that most of Hofmann's forgeries were only a few years old.

A highly magnified image of a ballpoint pen writing on paper. One way to figure out the age of a document is to measure the absorption of the ink by the paper.

41

THE MAN WHO WASHED STAMP PAPERS

Abdul Karim Telgi came from a poor family in southern India. He paid his own way through school before becoming a master forger. By the time he was finally caught, he was a millionaire.

Abdul Karim Telgi made a fortune out of forging stamp papers. His monthly profits were estimated at $20 million.

A typical stamp paper

STAMP PAPERS

In India, official "stamp papers" have to be used for every legal transaction. They must be bought from government offices. Abdul Karim Telgi discovered a way to wash used stamp papers clean and turn them into new papers. His network of 300 salespeople then sold the new papers at lower-than-normal prices. He even sold discounted stamps to big corporations, including Indian Oil and Life Insurance Corporation.

This is a voiceprint of a person saying the word "baby." The print would look different if another person said the word.

EXPOSED

Telgi's crimes were exposed when his organization sold papers to a lawyer without giving an official receipt. The lawyer complained, and the government realized that the stamp papers were not genuine.

TELGI'S EMPIRE COLLAPSES

The police began to **tap** Telgi's phone, hoping to find out more. What they heard amazed them: Telgi's empire of crime spread across a huge area of southern India. Telgi was quickly arrested. Voice analysis was used to prove that it had been him speaking in the phone calls. Telgi was served a long prison sentence for fraud.

VOICE ANALYSIS

Peoples' voices are unique, just like their fingerprints. Voices are affected by, among other things, breathing, the shape of the mouth, the way the vocal cords work, and how a person uses his or her tongue and lips while speaking. Voice analysis turns key parts of a person's voice into a graphic called a voiceprint. More than 100 different measurements can be included in a voiceprint, making it possible for investigators to say for sure whose voice they are listening to.

TIME LINE

330 B.C. Aristotle of Greece is the first to study how handwriting is related to personality.

250 B.C. Eristratus of Greece notices that his patients' hearts beat faster if they tell lies—the basis of the first lie-detection test.

1590s Zacharias' and Janssen's development of the microscope makes possible the in-depth study of documents, including paper, ink, and handwriting.

1609 François Demelle of France publishes the first essay on examining suspect documents.

1622 Camillo Baldi of Italy writes the first scientific book about the study of handwriting.

1686 Professor Marcello Malpighi of Italy notes the different parts of the fingerprint (ridges, spirals, and loops).

1810 A chemical test for a particular kind of ink is developed in Germany, an early example of chemical testing of documents.

1828 William Nichol's invention of the polarized light microscope allows scientists to study transparent materials, such as ink, in far greater detail than was previously possible.

1880 Dr. Henry Faulds of Britain publishes an article suggesting that fingerprints could be used as a means of identification.

1883 Alphonse Bertillon of France develops a system of identifying people through a set of measurements of their body, such as the size of their head and shape of their ears.

1891 Argentina becomes the first country to use fingerprint identification in court cases.

1894	In France, Alfred Dreyfus is convicted of treason based on a mistaken handwriting analysis.
1896	Röntgen's discovery of X-rays makes it possible to analyze structures within materials, such as paper and paint.
1904	Geological evidence is used in a legal case for the first time, in Germany.
1910	The world's first crime laboratory is established at the University of Lyons, France.
1910	Albert S. Osborne of the United States publishes *Questioned Documents*, a guide to examining possible forgeries.
1941	Murray Hill of the United States begins to study voiceprint identification.
1953	James Watson and Francis Crick publish a paper identifying the structure of DNA, paving the way for DNA testing in criminal investigations.
1968	Researchers in Japan conclude that people's lip prints are as unique as their fingerprints.
1977	In the United States, the FBI begins to computerize fingerprint records—the first step towards an automatic fingerprint identification system.
1980	U.S. researchers discover a part of DNA that varies from person to person.
1984	British scientists develop DNA fingerprinting as a way of identifying people.
1987	In the UK, Colin Pitchfork becomes the first person to be convicted of a crime on the basis of DNA evidence.
1995	The world's first national DNA database is started in Britain.

GLOSSARY

ancestor
Somebody from whom someone else is directly descended.

apostle
In the Mormon Church, someone who is sent to serve as a special witness of Jesus Christ and also serves as a leader of the church.

aristocrats
People with a high social status, often wealthy landowners who are allied to the royal family.

binding
The materials that hold the pages of a book together.

canvases
Painting surfaces made by stretching cloth over a wooden frame.

cell
The smallest independently functioning unit in the structure of a living thing.

collaboration
Working together. During wartime, collaboration is often used to mean working with the enemy.

colorants
Chemicals used to add color.

communist
Believing in a political system in which the government controls property, trade, and production.

counterfeit
a fake copy of something that is passed off as the real thing

denounce
To criticize in public or accuse somebody of wrongdoing.

DNA
The chemical molecule that carries the information defining all the characteristics of an individual. DNA is present in almost all the body's cells, and each person has unique DNA.

endpapers
Blank pages at the start and finish of a book.

exhume
To dig up remains of a dead person from a grave.

fossil
The ancient remains of a plant or animal that have been preserved in rock over time.

fossilized
Turned into a fossil, or turned into stone.

fraud
The act of obtaining money or some other benefit by lying, cheating, or tricking someone.

genetic
Relating to genes, the chemical instruction manual found in the cells of every living organism.

geologists
People who study rocks and the physical characteristics of the land.

GPS
The Global Positioning System is a system of satellites that allows people to figure out exactly where they are on Earth.

hypnotized
To be put into a trance, a dazed state where you are not aware of what you are doing.

jury
A group of ordinary people whose job is to listen to a legal case and decide who the guilty party is.

looted
Stolen by people during a period of social breakdown, such as during a war.

moored
(Of a boat) tied to a jetty, a pier, or some other safe place.

Nazi
A member of the Nazi Party that ruled Germany from 1933 to 1945.

paleontologist
A person who studies dinosaur fossils.

petrified
Organic matter turned into stone by a process of minerals seeping into its cells.

prototypes
The first versions of a new product, built to see if it works or not.

replica
A copy or reproduction.

tap
To listen in on a phone conversation using electronic devices.

testified
Gave evidence in court.

tissue sample
A small piece of someone's body, such as a piece of skin or some other organ.

ultraviolet
Radiation (energy waves) with wavelengths shorter than visible light but longer than X-rays.

watermark
A design that is part of a piece of paper. On old papers, the watermark allows people to see who made it, when, and where.

World War II
A war involving many of the world's countries, that lasted from 1939 to 1945.

FURTHER INFORMATION

BOOKS
Ancient Coins Were Shaped Like Hams: And Other Freaky Facts About Coins, Bills, and Counterfeiting
by Barbara Seuling, Picture Window Books, 2008.

Bizarre, Creepy Hoaxes (Edge Books)
by Kelly Regan Barnhill, Capstone Press, 2009

Cons and Frauds (Criminal Investigations)
by Michael Benson, Chelsea House Publications, 2008

Fakes and Forgeries (Facts on File)
Suzanne Bell, Facts On File, 2009.

WEB SITES
www.sniggle.net/index.php
An entertaining look at some of history's greatest hoaxes, frauds, and forgeries.

www.sciencenewsforkids.org/articles/200412 15/Feature1.asp
Lots of information on the techniques forensic experts use to collect evidence, as well as the types of crimes they help solve.

INDEX